A WEE GUIDE TO

Scottish Ghosts and Bogles

HAUNTED PLACES TO STAY AT AND TO VISIT

MARTIN COVENTRY

GOBLINSHEAD

PRESTONGRANGE HOUSE

First published 2000
Updated reprint 2004, 2008, revised and reset 2015
© Martin Coventry 2000, 2004, 2015

Published by GOBLINSHEAD
The Tower, West Wing, Prestongrange House
Prestonpans EH32 9RP
01875 812003
goblinshead@sol.co.uk

British Library Cataloguing in Publication Data
A catalogue record for this book is available from the
British Library.

ISBN 978 1 899874 33 0

Wee Guides
**William Wallace • The Picts • Scottish History
Whisky • The Jacobites • Robert Burns
Prehistoric Scotland • Mary, Queen of Scots
Robert the Bruce
• Rob Roy MacGregor • Scottish Ghosts and Bogles
• St Margaret and Malcolm Canmore
• Flora MacDonald**

Disclaimer:

*The information contained in this Wee Guide to Scottish Ghosts and Bogles (the
"Material") is believed to be accurate at the time of printing, but no representation or
warranty is given (express or implied) as to its accuracy, completeness or correctness. The
author and publisher do not accept any liability whatsoever for any direct, indirect or
consequential loss or damage arising in any way from any use of or reliance on this
Material for any purpose.*

*While every care has been taken to compile and check all the information in this book, in
a work of this complexity it is possible that mistakes and omissions may have occurred. If
you know of any corrections, alterations or improvements, please contact the publishers
at the address above.*

Contents

Acknowledgements

Many thanks to Joyce Miller, including for the permission to use the photo of Airth Castle (p. 7), to Hilary Horrocks and Isla Robertson at The National Trust for Scotland for permission to use the illustrations of the ceiling of the ceiling at Crathes (p. 28) and the main turnpike stair of Fyvie (p. 51), to Graham Coe for the photographs of Glamis (p. 53) and Hermitage (p. 58), and Dorothy Miller for Stirling Castle (p. 81).

Thanks also to following for illustrations and/or information at the following:

- Airth Castle (p. 5, 6)

- Borthwick Castle (p. 11, 12)

- Braemar Castle (p. 14, 15)

- Busta House (p. 17)

- Cawdor Castle

- Comlongon Castle (p. 21, 22)

- Coylet Inn (p. 23)

- Dalhousie Castle (p. 30, 31)

- Delgatie Castle (p. 33, 34, 35)

- Dunnottar Castle (p. 37, 38)

- Dunrobin Castle

- Dunvegan Castle (p. 44)

- Eilean Donan Castle (p. 46, 47, 48)

- Glamis Castle

- Maryculter House (p. 63)

- Meldrum House (p. 65)

- Montrose Air Station Museum (p. 67)

- New Lanark (p. 69)

- Rosslyn Chapel (p. 71, 72)

- Roxburghe Hotel (p. 75)

- Shieldhill Castle (p. 77)

- Tibbie Shiel's Inn (p. 82)

- Traquair House (p. 84, 85)

- Tulloch Castle Hotel (p. 87)

Ardchattan Priory (p. 8, 9), Borthwick Castle (p. 10), Cawdor Castle (p. 19), Loch Eck (p. 24), Craignethan Castle (p. 25), Crathes Castle (p. 27), Dunnottar Castle (p. 38, 39), Dunrobin (p. 39), Duntulm (p. 41), Dunvegan Castle (p. 43), Trumpan Church (p. 45), Fyvie (p. 49), St Bridget's Kirk, Dalgety (p. 52), Glen More (p. 57), Hermitage (p. 60), Rosslyn Castle (p. 73, 74), Stirling (p. 79, 80), and St Mary's Loch (p. 83) by Martin Coventry.

How to Use the Book

• The map (pages 2-3) shows the location of all the sites mentioned in the book, and there is a list of all sites (page 4) with page number and maps references. The haunted sites follow, 34 in total, although further places are mentioned in the text. The sites (from page 5) are arranged alphabetically. The entries provide information about location and history of the building or site, before going on to describe the haunting. The final section covers opening, telephone, and websites. There are also some 60 photographs.

• Several intriguing photographs and security camera footage which may show apparitions are mentioned in the text. These can be found on the internet using appropriate searches.

Warning
While the information in this book was believed to be correct at time of going to press – and was checked, where possible, with the places mentioned – opening times and facilities, or other information, may differ from that included. All information should be checked before embarking on any journey. Inclusion in the text is no indication whatsoever that a site is open to the public or that it should be visited. Care should be taken when visiting any site. Inclusion or exclusion of any site should not be considered as a comment or judgement on that site. Locations on the maps are approximate.

Preface

Every self-respecting hotel, castle or historic house should have its own bogle. This wee book is a selection of some of my favourite haunted stories and favourite places to visit. There are 34 sites, at which you can either stay or visit – or in some cases do both. It should be said that all these places are worth visiting for their own sake, and none need an evil bogle to make them interesting or rewarding. This is also only a small selection of haunted places which can be visited.

While my experience of castles and historic houses is quite extensive, my experience of anything supernatural at any of these places is strictly limited. I have visited many windswept and desolate places, even as the light was failing, even in the dead of winter – yet was not troubled.

I would just say, however, that I have no wish to stay in a haunted room as I would not sleep very well, my mind filled with half-heard rattles and clicks and creaks. My imagination is much more potent at terrifying me than the supernatural. One set of visitors immediately left one of Scotland's most visited attractions because a previous guest had written in the visitor book that they had seen an apparition.

Some places are, however, distinctly creepy, while some that might seem so – or are well known for their ghosts – are welcoming in comparison. Mary King's Close is a wonderful place to visit but for me it was less than scary. Glamis and Fyvie, too, are stunning buildings with fascinating ghost stories, but I wasn't in the least bit frightened. I have also visited many places when there have been no other visitors, but again nothing.

Most ghost stories are reputed to take place at night, but in reality manifestations are just as likely to be during the day. My own experiences of the unexplained or supernatural have happened at the least expected times, never at night, and most have been in the most mundane of places. There has never been a sudden drop in temperature, nor have the hairs on my back ever risen in fear. The crypt at Rosslyn Chapel was particularly dark and brooding, but – being half a Sinclair myself – perhaps all those Sinclairs once laid out in full armour without coffins had infiltrated my subconscious. I also thought that the Green Room at Crathes Castle and the ruins of Ardchattan Priory had a cold and a little grim atmosphere.

The only truly unpleasant and frightening experience, however, I have had visiting any of the places in this book was in the toilets at Craignethan Castle – no joke intended. This on a fine spring day with the sun beating down. And without (then) even knowing that Craignethan is reputedly haunted, that the newer building in the courtyard which houses the toilets is said to have its own bogles.

Even then nothing much actually happened. All I got was a distinct impression I was being watched by unfriendly eyes, and that something was quite angry and was urging me to leave that place as soon as possible. That and my guide book ending up in the toilet bowl, still not quite sure how. Not the kind of place you would expect any kind of supernatural occurrence. Very strange.

MC, Prestongrange House, August 2015.

A WEE GUIDE TO
Scottish Ghosts and Bogles

MAP: SCOTTISH GHOSTS AND BOGLES

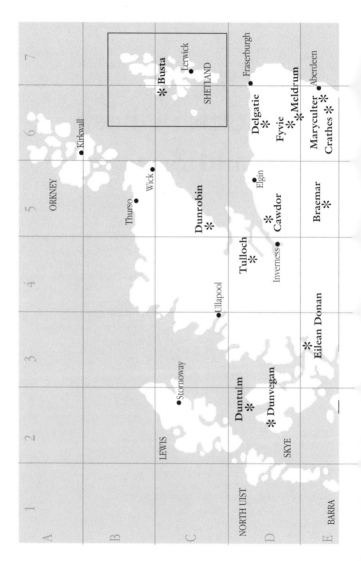

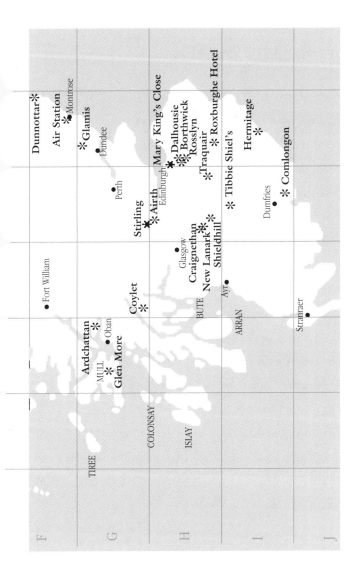

Dunnottar ✷

Air Station
✷ Montrose

✷ Glamis

● Dundee

● Perth

Stirling
✷ ✷ Airth
Edinburgh
Mary King's Close
✷ Dalhousie
✷ ✷ Borthwick
✷ Rosslyn
✷ Traquair
✷ Roxburghe Hotel

● Fort William

Glasgow ●

Coylet
✷

Craignethan
New Lanark ✷
Shieldhill

● Ayr

BUTE

ARRAN

✷ Tibbie Shiel's

Hermitage
✷

✷ Comlongon

● Dumfries

Ardchattan
✷

● Oban

MULL

Glen More
✷

COLONSAY

ISLAY

TIREE

● Stranraer

LIST OF HAUNTED SITES

Site (Map Ref)   *Page no*

Airth Castle

Off A905, 4 miles N of Falkirk, FK2 8JF.

Airth Castle is a small castle which incorporates much old work, including Wallace's Tower, a squat keep dating from

the 14th century. The castle was given a new castellated and towered front in the 19th century.

A stronghold here was held by a Fergus de Erth (Airth) in 1309. Airth saw action at end of the 14th century when William Wallace rescued his uncle, the Priest of Dunipace, from here after he had been imprisoned by the English.

Around 1470 Airth passed to the Bruces after Edward Bruce, second son of Robert Bruce of Clackmannan, married Agnes, daughter and heiress of William of Airth. Some 18 or so years later, in 1488, the castle was attacked and burned by James III. James was very unpopular with many of his unruly nobles, and he decided to punish the Bruces for rebelling against him. James, however, was soon defeated at the Battle of Sauchieburn, and assassinated after fleeing the field. Airth was restored with compensation from James IV, son of James III, who had led the rebel forces.

Airth was held by the Bruces until 1642, when it passed by marriage to the Elphinstones: several of the family are buried in the Airth aisle of the nearby ruinous Old Airth church. In 1717 the property was acquired by the Grahams whose descendants owned it until 1920. Since 1971 Airth has been used as a hotel and country club.

One room of the castle is said to be haunted by the ghost, perhaps a Green Lady, of a 17th-century housekeeper. The story goes that she neglected two children in her care, who were killed in a fire, and she cannot rest and still frantically searches the passages and chambers of Airth looking for them.

The unexplained sounds of children playing or running coming from empty rooms or corridors have also been reported.

An interesting photograph taken in 2007 of wedding

guests in the bar – and reported in the *Daily Record* – shows a fuzzy green apparition in the photo, possibly an image of the Green Lady.

Another story is of a bogle of a dog, felt rather seen, as guests and staff reported as if their ankles were being bitten.

A third tale is of a servant girl who was attacked by the laird, and her ghostly cries have also been reputedly heard.

And dusty footprints are also said to be left by the phantom of a groundsman.

Hotel.

Tel: 01324 831411

Web: www.airthcastlehotel.com

Ardchattan Priory

Off A828, 6.5 miles NE of Oban, Argyll, PA37 1RQ.

Standing in a scenic location on the north side of Loch Etive some miles from Oban is Ardchattan Priory. Much of the building is now ruinous and fragmentary, while other parts were incorporated into Ardchattan House. This was a Valliscaulian establishment dedicated to St Modan, and

founded in 1231 by Duncan MacDougall. Robert the Bruce is said to have held a parliament here in 1309, but the lands passed to the Campbells of Cawdor in 1602. The buildings were burnt in 1644, and again in 1654 by Cromwell's forces. The house was rebuilt and is still occupied.

The atmospheric ruins of the priory are in the care of Historic Scotland, and there are 16th-century carved grave slabs, burial aisles, a fine carved sarcophagus, and an early Christian carved wheel cross. The gardens of the adjacent Ardchattan House are also open to the public.

The priory ruins are said to be haunted by the ghost of a nun. The unexplained sounds of moaning and whispering have been reported, as well the phantom of the young girl.

She is said to have been the lover of one of the monks, who had repeated assignations with her lover. Fearing that their dalliance might eventually be discovered, they had agreed on a hiding place, an airless pit below the floor where she might conceal herself if they were in danger of being found together. Inevitably the prior appeared. She hid beneath the floor, but the prior knew of the hiding place and trapped her there, so that she died a prolonged and unpleasant death. The fate of her lover is not recorded…

Ruins of priory open at all reasonable times (Historic Scotland)

Gardens open April-October daily; house not open.

Tel: 01631 750274 (garden)

Web: www.ardchattan.co.uk

Carved sarcophagus, Ardchattan Priory.

BORTHWICK CASTLE

Off A7, 2 miles SE of Gorebridge, Midlothian, EH23 4QY.

One of the most impressive castles in Scotland, Borthwick
Castle is a magnificent looming U-plan tower house. It
consists of a double-towered keep, rising to 110 feet high
with walls up to 14 feet thick in places. The Great Hall is
one of the finest in the country and has a massive canopied
fireplace.

The bed chamber of Mary Queen of Scots.

The castle was built by Sir William Borthwick in 1430, who was given a licence to build the stronghold after he had been one of the hostages for the release of David II from captivity in England. The carved tomb with stone effigies of Borthwick and his wife is in nearby Borthwick Church.

The Borthwicks had long been prominent in Scottish affairs. One of the family had accompanied the heart of Robert the Bruce to Granada in Spain on crusade along with the Black Douglas and other Scottish nobles. Although the crusade was a disaster for the Scots, and many were slain, Borthwick distinguished himself by killing a Moorish chief and sticking his severed head on a pike. William, 4th Lord Borthwick, was slain at the Battle of Flodden in 1513 along with his king James IV.

Mary, Queen of Scots, and James Hepburn, Earl of Bothwell, stayed here in 1567. Bothwell was Mary's third husband, and was accused of being involved in the murder of Henry Stewart, Lord Darnley, who had been her previous husband. The couple were besieged in Borthwick and Mary had to escape, disguised as a pageboy. Little

11

then went right for her. She surrendered at the Battle of Carberry Hill shortly afterwards and was imprisoned in Lochleven Castle, where she was forced to abdicate in favour of her infant son, the future James VI. Although she escaped in 1568, her forces were defeated at the Battle of Langside and she fled to England. After being imprisoned there, she was finally executed in 1587.

It is recorded that her apparition, garbed as a pageboy, has been seen here.

Borthwick was more or less impregnable when it was built, but by the 17th century advances in cannon and gunpowder had made most castles redundant. In 1650 the castle was besieged by the forces of Oliver Cromwell as the then Lord Borthwick was holding out for the Royalists and Charles II. Borthwick was attacked with cannon and damage was done to the upper works and parapet. Lord Borthwick surrendered the castle, and was allowed to withdraw with his men and goods.

In this he was sensible: Tantallon Castle, one of the strongest fortresses in Scotland at that time, was reduced by Cromwell's forces in just 12 days.

The ghost story is both sad and cruel. A local girl, called Ann Grant, was apparently made pregnant by one of the Borthwick lords. The poor young woman, heavy with child, was seized, slashed across the abdomen with a sword, and then left to die in what is now the haunted room. This seems a particularly violent and vile crime, although also somewhat foolish and ill conceived.

This story seems to have come from when a modern visitor to the castle reported how he had seen a vision of the murder, as did a previous owner, although – it must be said – there seem to be no earlier reports of this particular tale so this, while certainly one of the most gruesome, is perhaps not the most credible of ghost stories.

Whatever the cause, guests, however, in one particular chamber reportedly experienced uncanny manifestations. The temperature in the chamber would suddenly drop, scratching was heard on the inside of the door. Footsteps were often heard on the turnpike stair from the room, around 1.30 am, when nobody was apparently about. A heavy fire door opened by itself one night and, during a business conference, weeping and wailing was heard, even although there was nobody in that part of the castle.

One of the previous owners allegedly had the haunted room exorcised, but apparently to no effect.

Another story is that of bogle of a chancellor of the castle, who was caught thieving money from the Borthwicks and was burned alive for his crimes.

Hotel.

Tel: 01875 820514

Web: borthwickcastle.com

Braemar Castle

On A93, 0.5 miles NE of Braemar, Deeside, AB35 5XR.

Located in a rugged, mountainous area of Scotland, Braemar Castle is an L-plan tower house, and stands in a strategic position. It replaced nearby Kindrochit Castle, which is said to have been destroyed by cannon when the inhabitants contracted the plague. Kindrochit is now a fragmentary ruin. One of the vaults, however, was broken in to during the Jacobite Rising of 1745-6 by Hanoverian soldiers seeking treasure. One of the searchers was confronted by a party of ghosts around a table piled with grinning skulls – or so it was reported.

Braemar Castle was built by the Erskine Earls of Mar in 1628, and was used both as a hunting lodge and to secure the area against the local clans of Farquharson, Forbes and Gordon. The castle has a massive iron yett, and an unlit and unventilated pit prison, which measures just 12 by

6 feet. The Farquharsons reoccupied and renovated the castle in the early 19th century.

The Earls of Mar supported William and Mary when the Stewart James VII was deposed in 1688. As a result the castle was captured and burned out by John Farquharson of Inverey, the 'Black Colonel', who was a staunch Jacobite. Farquharson, incidentally, summoned servants by firing a pistol, and his exploits evading government dragoons were legendary. He is said to haunt the castle, leaving behind a burning candle, and there is also a strange tale concerning his own death. The Black Colonel wished to be buried near his stronghold at Inverey, side by side with his mistress, but when he died he was interred at Braemar at the request of his widow and family. Apparently his spirit did not rest easy, and three times his coffin mysteriously appeared above ground – and his apparition also terrified his relatives – until they relented and his remains were taken back to Inverey.

Although the family had resisted the Jacobites, John, 11th Earl of Mar, led the 1715 Jacobite Rising. He was more of a politician than a soldier, however, and the rebellion fizzled out. Mar fled abroad and was stripped of his lands. The property passed to the Farquharsons of Invercauld, and was taken over by the government after the 1745-6 Jacobite Rising, refurbished, and turned into a barracks. The troops left in 1797, and castle was restored, and Queen Victoria visited when she attended the Braemar gathering.

One story is that Braemar is haunted the ghost of a young, blonde-haired woman, an innocent and shy lass.

A couple on their honeymoon were staying in the castle in the second half of the 19th century.

Early in the morning the husband left to go hunting, but his wife woke later, and, not knowing about the hunting, believed she had been abandoned, thinking that her new husband had not found the previous night to his satisfaction. In misery, the poor girl threw herself from the battlements.

Her ghost is said to haunt the castle, searching for her husband. The apparition reputedly was sighted in 1987, and it is thought that she only appears to those who have recently been married. Ghostly footsteps, the light tread of a woman, have also been reported.

Further reports of ghosts include a piper witnessed in the back corridor and the unexplained wailing of a phantom baby, allegedly from an infant murdered in the building.

Braemar Castle open April-October: April-June and September-October, Wednesday-Sunday; July-August daily.

Tel: 01339 741219

Web: www.braemarcastle.co.uk

Busta House

Off A970, 10 miles NW of Lerwick, Busta, Brae, Muckle Roe, Shetland, ZE2 9QN.

Located on Muckle Roe to the north of the mainland of Shetland is Busta (pronounced 'Boosta') House. It is a tall, harled and white-washed mansion, set in a picturesque,

tranquil location with its own harbour and extensive grounds. It is believed to date from 1588, but was remodelled and added to in 1714, and then again in 1984. It is now a comfortable and popular hotel.

Busta was owned by the Giffords of Busta, who held much property on Shetland. They were descended from a Scots minister, and made their fortunes as merchants and fish exporters. In 1714 Thomas Gifford married Elizabeth Mitchell. Gifford was wealthy and prominent in Shetland, and was made Steward Depute, as well as Chamberlain. But tragedy was to follow.

Gifford had four sons, but on 14 May 1748 they were all

tragically drowned in a boating accident on Busta Voe. This left Gifford without a male heir, until Barbara Pitcairn, a pretty maid (or guest depending in the version) in the house, said that she had been secretly married to John, the oldest son, and was pregnant by him. She had papers to prove the marriage, and when she had a son, Gideon, he was adopted as Gifford's heir. Barbara was shunned, however, and forced to leave Busta. She died at just 36 in the house of a poor relation in Lerwick. It is said that her sad ghost haunts the building, searching for her son. A young child reported seeing a lady in the bar, and tried to offer her food. The people with him saw nobody. On the hotel website it mentions that Barbara's apparition is frequently seen by guests.

Gideon himself had no direct heirs, and the resulting lawsuits about who should inherit the property left the estate in financial difficulties.

It would appear, however, that it is not just Barbara who haunts Busta. There have been several sightings of an apparition in the Linga room. The ghost is said to be a grey-haired woman, in a brown dress and lace cap, and the visitations have been recorded by several different guests on separate occasions. It does not appear to be Barbara as she was young when she died, and it may be Elizabeth Mitchell, wife of Thomas Gifford.

Other manifestations include the sound of heavy footsteps coming from the Foula Room when unoccupied, reported by a guest in the room below. Lights and other electrical equipment have also turned themselves off and on. Disturbances are said to be more prevalent in May, around the anniversary of the death of Gifford brothers.

Hotel.

Tel: 01806 522506

Web: www.bustahouse.com

Cawdor Castle

Off B9090, 5 miles SW of Nairn, Highlands, IV12 5RD.

A magnificent and well-preserved stronghold, Cawdor Castle incorporates a tall 14th-century keep with later ranges around a courtyard. There are many fine furnished rooms, and there is a magnificent garden.

The title 'Thane of Cawdor' is associated with Macbeth, but King Duncan was not murdered here – the castle is not nearly old enough – as he was killed in battle near Spynie. The 1st Thane of Cawdor took the name of Calder when granted the lands by Alexander II in 1236, although one story is that the family were descended from a brother of Macbeth. The 3rd Thane was murdered by Sir Alexander Rait of nearby Rait Castle.

Rait Castle has its own gruesome ghost story.

In 1524 the Mackintoshes were invited to Rait to witness the marriage of the laird's daughter to one of their number. The plan was, however, to slay the Mackintoshes at the

feast. Unfortunately for the laird, his plan was discovered and the Mackintoshes were heavily armed and weighed into the fight. The laird lost many of his own men.

He suspected his daughter of betraying the plot, as she was in love with her intended husband. In a rage he pursued the terrified girl through the castle. She attempted to escape from an upstairs window, climbed out, and was hanging from the window sill when her father caught her. He hacked off her hands at the wrist with his sword and the poor girl fell to her death.

Her ghost, a handless phantom clad in a blood-spattered wedding dress, is said to still haunt Rait.

The method of selecting the site for Cawdor Castle was a little unusual, even unique, as it was chosen by a wandering donkey. Cawdor is also built over a tree, the remains of which are in the vaulted basement. It was long believed to be a hawthorn, but in fact it proved to be a holly tree, which died in about 1372, when the castle was built.

The Campbells acquired Cawdor by abducting the infant heiress Muriel Calder in 1511 and marrying her to Sir John Campbell, son of the Earl of Argyll. The six sons of Campbell of Inverliver were slain during the abduction. The Campbells of Cawdor still own the castle.

Cawdor has a couple of ghost stories. An apparition of a lady in a blue velvet dress has reputedly been seen here, as has a phantom of John Campbell, 1st Lord Cawdor.

Open May-mid October, daily.

Tel: 01667 404401

Web: www.cawdorcastle.com

COMLONGON CASTLE

Off B724, 8 miles SE of Dumfries.

Standing in 120 acres of secluded woodland and gardens, Comlongon Castle consists of a massive keep, with walls 14 feet thick in places, to which a mansion was added in

the 19th century. The grand hall has a massive fireplace, and there is a dark pit prison.

Comlongon was held by the Murray family from 1331 until 1984, and the family became Earls of Annandale, and later of Mansfield. The building is now a hotel.

The castle is believed to be haunted by a Green Lady, the bogle of Marion Carruthers of Mouswald. She was the joint heir to her father's wealthy lands of Mouswald after he was killed in a raid. Marrying her would mean that her husband would acquire her father's castles and lands. She seems to have been a feisty lass, but (sadly for her) with the Douglases as guardians.

The unwilling girl was forced into a betrothal of marriage with Sir James Douglas of Drumlanrig – or to John MacMath, his nephew, depending on the version of the story. Either way, she was to marry a man she did not love, although the motive appears to have been to seize

her lands rather than any desire for Marion herself.

Marion fled to Comlongon, her uncle's castle. Even the Privy Council seemed to be against her and in 1563 ordered her into the wardenship of Borthwick Castle. Although she was sheltered in Comlongon by the then laird, Sir William Murray, she was so distressed from the long dispute that she committed suicide by jumping from the lookout tower. This part is well documented from the time.

An alternative version is that she was murdered by the Douglases, who gained access to her room and threw her from the roof. Because she was thought to have committed suicide, she was not given a Christian burial. It is said no grass will grow on the spot where the poor girl died. This happened on 25 September 1570.

Her apparition, a forlorn sobbing girl, is said to have been witnessed, both in the grounds and castle. The sounds of her weeping have also been heard, and a ghostly presence, which has pushed past people, has also been recorded. Some say that she searches for a proper resting place as she was not given a Christian burial. An apparition appears to be shown on a photo of the great hall.

Hotel. Wedding venue.

Tel: 01387 870283

Web: www.comlongon.com

Coylet Inn

On A815, Loch Eck, 8 miles N of Dunoon, Argyll, PA23 8SG.

Standing on the banks of scenic Loch Eck, the Coylet Inn is a small family-run country hotel, and dates from the

17th century. It is set in a picturesque area, surrounded by the Argyll Forest Park, and the area offers hill walking, pony trekking, sea angling and boat hire on the loch.

The inn is believed to be haunted by the 'Blue Boy', the apparition of a young lad who returns to find his mother. Objects have mysteriously disappeared from one area only to reappear in another. Staff have also reported wet footprints when nobody has been present to make them.

The story goes that a young lad staying at Coylet on occasion walked in his sleep. One night in a dream he left the hotel, crossed the road, and wandered down into Loch Eck. He was drowned in the cold water, leaving his body

Loch Eck, from near the Coylet Inn.

chill and blue. It is thought to be his ghost which causes the disturbances, and the story was incorporated into a film in 1994.

Sadly the inn suffered a serious fire in July 2015.

Hotel.

Tel: 01369 840426

Web: www.thecoyletinn.co.uk

CRAIGNETHAN CASTLE

Off A72, 4.5 miles W of Lanark, ML11 9PL.

Craignethan is a grand and imposing ruin, set on top of a wooded ravine. It was built to withstand artillery and is arranged around a squat tower house, formerly with a massively thick bastion, curtain walls and corner towers. There is a caponier, a small vaulted building built to defend the bottom of the ditch.

Craignethan was built by Sir James Hamilton of Finnart in 1532. Hamilton was the illegitimate son of the 1st Earl of Arran, and a talented architect and acquisitive subject. For many years he was in favour with James V, but latterly fell out with his monarch, and was beheaded for treason in 1540. The king retained his lands and the castle of Craignethan. Within two years, however, James V was dead and the property reverted to the Hamiltons.

James, 2nd Earl of Arran, was a very powerful man, and acquired the castle. He was Regent for Mary, Queen of Scots, and the Hamiltons continued to support her as she became increasingly unpopular. She may have spent

one or more nights here before the Battle of Langside in 1568, although several other places have been suggested – one of the chambers in the castle was known as the Queen's Room. The Hamiltons formed the main part of her army, but were defeated by the Regent Moray, and the castle was seized. Mary withdrew to England where she was eventually executed by beheading. A headless ghost dressed in white has been reported here, identified by some as the spirit of Mary. This is by no means the only castle she is said to haunt: Stirling, Hermitage, Borthwick and Lochleven are a few of the others.

Although the defeat at Langside was disastrous, the Hamiltons rallied and retook the castle. But by 1579 their position was untenable and they abandoned Craignethan, which was then slighted and the defences partly demolished – although it continued to be a residence. A later house was also built in the corner of the outer courtyard.

Other ghosts are said to have been witnessed in this later house, where the unexplained voices of women have been heard, and a vague shifting apparition seen. Items have also been mysteriously moved around.

The phantom of a woman wearing Stuart-period dress was witnessed in the courtyard in recent times. The apparition was followed by two visitors who did not realise it was a ghost until it faded away.

Other unexplained manifestations include pipe music.

Historic Scotland: open Apr-Sep, daily.

Tel: 01555 860364

CRATHES CASTLE

Off A93, 3 miles E of Banchory, Kincardine & Deeside, AB31 5QJ.

Crathes is one of the most outstanding castles in Scotland. The lower part of the massive tower is plain, while the upper storeys have a plethora of corbelling, turrets, and stone decoration. The castle has many fine furnished

apartments, some with magnificent original painted ceilings, including the Green Lady's Room and the Room of the Nine Muses. There is a walled garden, covering nearly four acres, with eight separate areas of unusual plants, including the Fountain Garden, Rose Garden and Wild Garden.

Painted ceiling, Crathes.

The Burnetts of Leys held the property from the 14th century, and they built Crathes Castle around 1553. They owned the stronghold and estate for some 400 years until it passed in 1952 to The National Trust for Scotland. The ivory and jewel-bedecked Horn of Leys was given to the family by Robert the Bruce in 1323 and is on display in the High Hall of Crathes.

Crathes is said to have a Green Lady, seen or witnessed down the centuries. The ghost was so active that the chamber where she mostly frequents is now called the Green Lady's Room. This a chamber on the third floor of the tower, and was originally a bedroom. As is usual with ghost stories, there are several versions of the legend of the bogle. The phantom, usually described as wearing a green dress, reportedly first appeared in the 18th century, and is seen crossing the floor, with a baby in her arms.

The young woman seems to have been a daughter of

the then laird or, in the story in the guide book, a lass in his protection. She had been cavorting with a servant or was cruelly used by a retainer of the laird.

What is agreed, however, is that the poor girl was made pregnant and gave birth. It appears that the baby, at least, was then murdered or perhaps the wee thing died of natural causes, but then was concealed in the room. A skeleton of an infant was found by workmen in a small recess under the hearthstone during renovations in the 19th century.

The Green Lady traditionally appeared when a death or misfortune was to befall the resident family.

The apparition, again with baby, was reportedly seen by Queen Victoria. The haunted room was unpopular with guests as they described feeling extremely uneasy or tense or that there was a strange presence there.

The phantom is said to have been witnessed often, even in recent times, as mentioned above wearing a green frock with a baby in her arms, but also described as 'being like a luminous block of ice, not human shaped, but it moved as if someone was walking'. There was also a small apparition accompanying the larger luminous shape. In this particular case, the appearance is said to have occurred with a pronounced drop in temperature.

Even now some visitors to Crathes apparently refuse to enter the Green Lady's Room without knowing the story, while a guide is said to have felt something or someone brush past her when there was nothing there.

NTS: open April-October, daily; November-March, Tuesday-Sunday: check festive period. Grounds and garden open all year.

Tel: 01330 844525

Web: www.nts.org.uk

Dalhousie Castle

Off B704, Bonnyrigg, 3 miles S of Dalkeith, Midlothian, EH19 3JB.

Dalhousie Castle, which is situated in acres of forest, park land and river pasture, is an imposing castle and mansion with battlements and turrets. It incorporates an ancient stronghold with a drum tower, but was altered and

extended in following centuries. It still retains many original features, such as the slots for the drawbridge, a turnpike stair, and the bottle dungeon into which prisoners were lowered by a rope. It is now a fine hotel.

The castle was built by the Ramsays, who came to Scotland with David I in the 12th century. Sir Alexander Ramsay was active in the Wars of Independence, and captured Roxburgh Castle from the English. In 1342 he was starved to death in Hermitage Castle. Ramsay's ghost is believed to haunt Hermitage.

Dalhousie withstood a siege by the English in 1400, which lasted six months, although the then laird was killed only two years later at Homildon Hill, while another was

slain at the Battle of Flodden in 1513. The family supported Mary Queen of Scots, and fought for her at Langside in 1568. The family were later made Earls of Dalhousie, and Oliver Cromwell visited the castle in 1648.

The Ramsays lived at the castle until about 1900, when they moved to Brechin Castle in Angus, and in 1925 the castle became a boys' private school. This was closed in 1950, and some 20 years later the castle was converted into a hotel. The castle features many individually designed bedrooms and the barrel-vaulted Dungeon Restaurant.

Dalhousie is said to be haunted by a Grey Lady, the phantom of young Lady Catherine. The tale is that she was the mistress of one of the Ramsays, possibly around the turn of the 17th century. Ramsay's wife found out about Catherine, and had her imprisoned in one of the castle turrets, where she died from starvation. Lady Catherine's remains are said to be walled up somewhere in the building, although whether this was to kill her or conceal her body after she was dead is not clear. An alternative version is that she was a 16-year-old daughter of the house and was found canoodling with a stable lad

Her apparition has allegedly been often seen on the stairs of the castle, in the dungeons, and along the 'Black' corridor, which was originally battlements of the old stronghold. The apparition is said to have sharp features, and to be clad in a grey dress with puff sleeves and to have small feet in pointed shoes. Some guests seem to have thought the phantom was a member of staff until she disappeared through a locked door. Other reported manifestations include the rustling of a gown, and scratching or tapping at doors. An apparition was seen in one of the bedrooms in 2000, and in 2013 a guest reported the unexplained sounds of a woman gasping and the feeling of silk being drawn across her ankles. There is also an intriguing photo from wedding celebrations in 2004, apparently showing an apparition…

Another ghost is said to be that of one of the pupils from when the castle was a school. The story goes that a boy leapt from the top of the building and was killed.

A third spirit is that of a dog, which died in the 1980s after also falling from the castle. Its apparition has allegedly been seen running on the stairs and along the passageways.

Other reported manifestations include a member of staff having her hair pulled when nobody else was present, and a guest being tapped on each shoulder several times by invisible hands.

Hotel.

Tel: 01875 820153

Web: dalhousiecastle.co.uk

DELGATIE CASTLE

Off A947, 2 miles E of Turriff, Banff & Buchan, AB53 6TD.

Set in a fine location, Delgatie Castle is an ancient and interesting pile with walls up to 14 feet thick in places. The main tower rises to five storeys and over 60 feet, and there are fine original painted ceilings of the 16th century and a massive turnpike stair.

There was a stronghold here from 1050, and it was captured from the Comyn Earl of Buchan by Robert the Bruce. The lands were given to the Hays by Bruce in the 14th century, and they held them for some 350 years. The family were made Earls of Errol in 1452, and Mary, Queen of Scots, spent three days here in 1562. Francis, 9th Earl,

Rohaise's room.

was accused of treason in 1594, and part of the west wall was demolished by James VI's forces. Sir William Hay was standard bearer to the famous Marquis of Montrose. Although defeated at Philiphaugh, Hay managed to return the Marquis's standard to Buchanan Castle. Hay was later captured and then executed at Edinburgh in 1650, and buried beside Montrose in St Giles Cathedral. The family supported the Jacobites in both the 1715 and 1745 Risings.

The castle had to be sold in 1762, and was occupied by the army during the last war. It was then left uninhabited until bought back by the Hays who began the task of restoration.

Delgatie is said to be haunted by a the ghost of a red-haired and spirited young lass, called Rohaise. She is thought to have defended the castle when it was being attacked, although how she died is not recorded. Her bogle mostly haunts the bedroom off the main stair, which is now called Rohaise's Room. It is said she especially likes to visit men who stay in the chamber.

The ghost was frightening enough to have troops

Painted 16th-century ceiling.

stationed here during World War II flee outside following unexplained disturbances on at least two occasions. A search of the building found nothing, of course.

There are also stories of a ghostly monk, whose body had been walled up in the castle.

Open all year, except closed for two weeks over Xmas. B&B. Holiday accommodation. Fishing. Weddings.

Tel: 01888 563479

Web: www.delgatiecastle.com

Dunnottar Castle

Off A92, 2 miles S of Stonehaven, Kincardine & Deeside, AB39 2TL.

Set on a virtually impregnable cliff-top promontory some 160 feet above the sea, Dunnottar Castle is simply one of the most spectacular and photogenic castles in Scotland. External shots of the castle were used in the film version of *Hamlet* with Mel Gibson.

There was a stronghold here from early times, and it was besieged by the Picts, and then in 900 by Vikings when Donald King of Scots was slain. The present castle was built by the Keith Earls Marischal who held the property until 1716 when they were forfeited for their part in the Jacobite Rising. Famous visitors include Mary Queen of Scots, Charles II, and the great freedom fighter William Wallace. Wallace captured Dunnottar in 1296 and is said to have burnt 4000 Englishmen, at least according to Blind Harry writing many years later.

In 1651 the Scottish crown and regalia were taken to

Dunnottar as Cromwell's invasion of Scotland advanced northwards. His army reached Dunnottar in 1652 and besieged the castle. This proved extremely difficult, and the castle was only reduced after eight months by starvation and mutiny. Before the garrison surrendered, however, the regalia and state papers were smuggled out and hidden in nearby Kinneff Church until they were recovered at the Restoration of Charles II.

Some 30 years later, more than 150 Covenanters were imprisoned in one of the vaults in appalling conditions, and nine died while 25 managed to escape down the cliffs. One tale is that ghostly cries can be heard coming from the vault…

Sightings of several ghosts have also been reported here. The apparition of a girl, around 13 years old and dressed in a dull plaid-type dress, perhaps green, is said to have been witnessed in the brewery. She leaves by the doorway next to the building, but then vanishes.

Other ghosts are said to include a young deer hound,

Main entrance and guard room.

which faded away near the tunnel, a tall Scandinavian-looking man going into the guardroom at the main entrance, who then also vanished, and noises of a meeting coming from Benholm's Lodging when nobody was apparently present.

Open all year, daily except closed 25 and 26 December and 1 and 2 January. Steep walk to castle and steeper back.

Tel: 01569 762173 (kiosk)

Web: www.dunnottarcastle.co.uk

Dunrobin Castle

Off A9, 1.5 miles NE of Golspie, Sutherland, KW10 6SF.

Set in fine policies overlooking the North Sea, Dunrobin dates from the 1300s and is a splendid fairytale castle with a mass of turrets and spires. It was extended and

remodelled about 1650, 1780 and in 1845-50, and has some 189 rooms. There are beautiful formal gardens, designed by Charles Barry, architect of the Houses of Parliament.

The family became Earls of Sutherland in 1235, and had a castle here from the 13th century: Dunrobin may be called after Robert or Robin, 6th Earl. The family were made Dukes of Sutherland in 1832, but are not always fondly regarded because of their active and prominent role in the Highland Clearances.

The upper floors of the old part of the castle are reputedly haunted by the bogle of Margaret, daughter of John Gordon, 14th Earl of Sutherland.

Around the end of the 17th century, she fell for Jamie Gunn, younger son of one of the Earl's men. But her father found out, and had her imprisoned in one of the attic rooms so that nothing improper could happen. Margaret despaired and Gunn decided to rescue her by smuggling a rope to her. Margaret tried to climb down out of one of the windows, but her father burst into her room, startling her so much that she let go of the rope and fell to her death.

A different account is that the lass was a pretty Mackay girl that the Earl of Sutherland had taken a fancy to and had carried off to Dunrobin. Here, he imprisoned her in the upstairs room, hoping to make her his. This was not to her liking and she tried to escape down a rope from the window. The Earl arrived just as she had begun her descent, and cut the rope with his sword, so that the unfortunate girl was dashed to death on the ground below.

It is said that – at least on occasion – that one of the haunted rooms was abandoned, and unexplained moans and cries still come from the chamber where the poor lass was imprisoned. Unexplained footsteps have also allegedly been heard, including in the Clan Society Room and the Drawing Room.

There is also an account of the phantom of a man being witnessed, before being seen to vanish through a closed door.

Open April-mid October, daily.

Tel: 01408 633177

Web: www.dunrobincastle.co.uk

Duntulm Castle

Off A855, 6.5 miles N of Uig, Skye.

Located in a beautiful spot on the northern tip of the lovely island of Skye, Duntulm Castle stands on a cliff-girt headland, looking out over the Little Minch to the Outer Hebrides. Unfortunately, little survives of the castle, once

the fine stronghold of the MacDonalds, which welcomed James V, sadly allowed to go to utter ruin. The family moved to Monkstadt from here about 1730, reputedly because of the many ghosts at Duntulm. They later built Armadale in Sleat, to the south of the island, where the Clan Donald Centre is now located, although the mansion is ruinous after a fire.

There was a stronghold at Duntulm from early times, and it was taken by Vikings and called Dun David. When this part of Scotland finally came under the control of the kings of Scots in the 13th century, a medieval fortress was built here. The territory was fought over by the MacLeods, from their own stronghold of Dunvegan, and MacDonalds of Sleat, the latter finally gaining the ascendancy.

At the turn of the 17th century, Hugh MacDonald, cousin to the then chief, Donald Gorm Mor (himself not an especially nice fellow), plotted to gain the lands. Donald Gorm had no heirs, and Hugh planned to invite the chief to his own fortress, Caisteal Uisdean, some miles south of Duntulm, and there murder him. Unfortunately for him, he mixed up letters sent to the chief and to the proposed assassin. Hugh then fled to North Uist, where he was besieged at Dun an Sticar, to the north of that island. Hugh was captured, and imprisoned in a vault at Duntulm. He was given salted beef and no water, and is reported to have died insane and raving from thirst and dehydration. When the vault was finally opened, his skeleton still grasped an empty jug in its parched jaws. His bones were kept as a warning to others in a local church, and his ghostly groans have reputedly been heard here since.

The boisterous ghost of the chief, Donald Gorm Mor, riotously partying with spectral companions, has also been recorded in many tales, and in some is given as the reason the MacDonalds left Duntulm.

Another apparition was said to be that of Margaret, a sister of MacLeod of Dunvegan, and Donald's wife. She had lost an eye in an accident, so her husband threw her out, sending her back to Dunvegan on a one-eyed horse with a one-eyed servant and one-eyed dog. Her weeping ghost is said to haunt the castle.

A nursemaid is said to have dropped a baby out of one of the windows, onto the rocks far below. Her terrified screams are said to be heard sometimes as the poor woman was cruelly slain in revenge.

View from exterior – dangerously ruined.

DUNVEGAN CASTLE

Off A850, 1 mile N of Dunvegan, Skye, IV55 8WF.

Set on what was once an island to the north of the beautiful island of Skye, Dunvegan Castle has been continuously occupied by the chiefs of MacLeod since 1270. The clan trace their ancestry back to Leod, a son of Olaf the Black, Viking king of the Isle of Man. His old stronghold was remodelled down the centuries into a large and comfortable castle and mansion, and Dunvegan is now owned by Hugh MacLeod, 30th Chief of MacLeod.

Dunvegan is home to the legendary Fairy Flag, which is on display at the castle, and is known as *Am Bratach Sith* in Gaelic. The flag is actually a piece of silk, now greatly reduced in size and somewhat tattered as down the years pieces were removed and kept for luck.

The legend is that the flag was given to a MacLeod chief by his wife when they parted at the Fairy Bridge, three miles to the north east, at a meeting of rivers and roads. The chief had married his wife thinking she was a mortal woman, but she was actually a fairy and was only allowed

Fairy Flag.

to stay with him for 20 years before returning to her home.

That is the legend. The silk that the flag is made from, however, originates from the Middle East. This has been dated between 400 and 700 AD, older than the present castle by hundreds of years. The flag is believed to give victory to the clan whenever unfurled (or three times, anyway), and reputedly did so at the battles of Glendale in 1490 and at Trumpan in 1580.

The Battle at Trumpan is one of the more notorious events in the long clan battles between the MacLeods and the MacDonalds. At Trumpan, some miles east of Dunvegan, worshippers were at the church one Sunday in 1578. A raiding party of MacDonalds came ashore. They set fire to the thatched roof of the church, and most of the worshippers – men, women and children – were burnt alive or slain. One woman escaped, raising the alarm at Dunvegan.

Trumpan Church.

The MacLeods gathered a small force, bringing with them the Fairy Flag. The MacDonalds were then the ones who were slaughtered after the Flag was unfurled. On the anniversary of the massacre in the church, it is said that the singing of the ghostly congregation at Trumpan can be heard.

The Fairy Flag was also believed to make the marriage bed fecund when draped over it, and to charm the herrings out of the sea. Belief in its power was so enduring that in World War II pilots carried a picture of the flag for luck. There is no record whether this worked or not…

There are stories that at times unexplained eerie music can be heard coming from the chamber at Dunvegan in which the flag is on display. The ghostly skirl of bagpipes has also been reported from one of the towers.

Dunvegan Castle open April-mid October, daily.

Tel: 01470 521206

Web: www.dunvegancastle.com

Eilean Donan Castle

On A87, 8 miles E of Kyle of Lochalsh, Highland.

In a lovely spot surrounded by water and mountains, Eilean Donan Castle is possibly the most photogenic of all Scottish strongholds. Although ruinous, it was completely

rebuilt between 1912 and 1932. A strong tower, with walls up to 15 feet thick, and a courtyard and other buildings stand on a small island, now linked to the mainland by a bridge. Several movies used the castle as a location, including *Highlander*, *Loch Ness*, and *James Bond*.

There may have been an early community of monks here, and the island is named after the 6th-century saint from Ireland St Donan. Eilean Donan was long held by the Mackenzies, and it was here that Robert the Bruce sheltered in 1306. In 1331 Thomas Randolph, Earl of Moray, executed 50 men and spiked their heads on the castle walls. In 1511 the MacRaes became constables of the castle for the Mackenzies, and in 1539 the castle was besieged by Donald Gorm MacDonald who was claiming the Lordship of the Isles.

Banqueting Hall.

Only two men were left to defend the castle, and with their last arrow they shot Donald Gorm, but only hit him in the foot. Donald Gorm quickly pulled out the arrow, but in so doing severed an artery and soon died. The half-hearted siege which followed was soon abandoned.

The MacRaes and Mackenzies were Jacobites, and suffered heavy casualties at the Battle of Sheriffmuir in 1715. William Mackenzie, 5th Earl of Seaforth, garrisoned Eilean Donan with Spanish troops in the Rising of 1719. Three Government frigates attacked the castle and it was soon surrendered. The powder magazine was then ignited, some 343 barrels of gunpowder, blowing the castle apart.

The Spaniards, about 300 men along with a force of Scottish Jacobites, were soon defeated by government troops at the nearby Battle of Glenshiel. The site is marked by an information board.

The castle is said to be haunted by the headless bogle of one of the Spanish troops, either killed at Eilean Donan or at the Battle of Glenshiel. His ghost, of course, carries his head under his arm, and is said to have been witnessed in the gift shop.

Another apparition, the ghost of Lady Mary, reputedly haunts one of the bedrooms.

Open Apr-Oct, daily 10.00-17.30.

Tel: 01599 555202

Web: www.eileandonan.co.uk

Fyvie Castle

Off A947, 8 miles SE of Turriff and 1 mile N of Fyvie village, Fyvie, Banff & Buchan, AB53 8JS.

Set in the green and rolling countryside of Aberdeenshire, Fyvie Castle is a grand and imposing building, adorned with turrets, corbelling, dormer windows, carved finials, and corbiestepped gables. Down the centuries the building was developed from a fortress into a comfortable and

striking stately home, and has a fine Edwardian interior.

Thomas the Rhymer is recorded as having made a prophecy concerning Fyvie and the 'weeping stones'. When the castle was first being built, a nearby chapel was demolished and the materials brought towards Fyvie, but these fell into the river. The then laird refused Thomas shelter in the castle, and the Rhymer is said to have foretold that unless all three stones were found the castle and lands would never descend in direct line for more than two generations. Only two of the stones were found. One is on display in the charter room, while another is reported to be built into the foundations. These stones are said to 'weep', oozing with water, when tragedy is going to strike.

Fyvie was certainly destined to have a succession of owners. The property was originally held by the Crown, but it was given to the Lindsays in 1370, and then passed to the Prestons in 1402, then about 1433 to the Meldrums, then the Seton Earls of Dunfermline in 1596, then to the Gordon Earls of Aberdeen in 1733 and finally to the Leith family in 1889. The castle was put onto the open market in 1982, and is now owned by The National Trust for Scotland.

The castle is reputedly haunted by a Green Lady, believed by many to be the ghost of Lilias Drummond.

Lilias was the daughter of Patrick Drummond, 3rd Lord Drummond, and was married at about 17 or 18 to Alexander Seton, then owner of Fyvie, by then in his mid 30s. Lilias had five daughters over the next ten or so years, four of whom survived into adulthood, although there may have been other pregnancies. Her husband presumably wanted a son and heir, but this was not to happen as Lilias died on 8 May 1601, at about the age of 30, at Dalgety, Seton's house in Fife. She was buried in the Seton family vault at St Bridget's Church.

One theory is that she was starved to death by her husband, another that she may have died of a broken heart, or perhaps she simply grew ill and died – as in many stories details are confused. Whatever the truth of it, Seton married Grizel Leslie only six months after Lilias's death – in fact he was contracted to Grizel within a few weeks.

On their wedding night, 27 October, Seton and his new wife were staying in what is now known as the Drummond Room. They were plagued all night by sighing coming from the window, and in the morning the following was found carved into the window sill, some 50 feet from the ground:

'D[ame] LILLIES DRUMMOND'. Although this seems far fetched, the writing can still be seen and it is an unusual place for anyone to have their name carved, particularly as it faces outward. The ghost is recorded as being seen often on the main turnpike stair from the 17th century onwards, and a document from the time mentions a 'Green Ladye'.

Grizel died some five years later, again without a son, but Seton married again, and this time had an heir, Charles. By then he had been Chancellor of Scotland and was made Earl of Dunfermline in 1606. He died in 1622.

In the 19th century Colonel Cosmo Gordon recorded that he had been shaken out of bed by invisible hands, and on another night a wind arose which blew the covers off several beds including his own. Lilias is thought to have appeared before the death of Cosmo in 1879, and Alexander Gordon a few years later.

The ghost has been described on occasion as both a flickering glow or a shifting patch of light, but also as a shining phantom in a green dress with a candle in her hands and pearls in her hair.

The castle is also reported to have a Grey Lady, believed to be the spirit of a lady starved to death here, perhaps a

Main turnpike stair, Fyvie.

51

confusion or conflation with Lilias. The ghost was at its most active in the 1920s and 1930s. When workmen were renovating the gun room in the castle, they found a secret chamber in which they uncovered the remains of a woman. When the skeleton was removed, disturbances increased until the bones were returned – or so it is said.

Some say the castle also has a ghostly drummer, while others mention a trumpeter, the ghost of Andrew Lammie. He is said to have fallen in love with Agnes, daughter of a local miller, but her parents had him banished or abducted. His ghost is said to return and blow a trumpet when one of the resident family is near death.

NTS: open April-October, Saturday-Wednesday; June-August, daily. Garden, open all year.

Tel: 01651 891266

Web: www.nts.org.uk

St Bridget's Kirk, Dalgety – Lilias Drummond is buried here.

GLAMIS CASTLE

Off A94, 5.5 miles SW of Forfar, Angus, DD8 1RJ.

Nestling in set in fine park land with an Italian garden, Glamis Castle is a magnificent and stately building, but is

probably best known as one of the most (reputedly) haunted places in Britain.

The huge keep towers above the area with an extravagant flourish of corbelling, sculpture, turrets and pinnacles crowning the building. A wide turnpike stair climbs 143 steps from the basement to the battlements, and the keep is vaulted on three floors, housing 'Duncan's Hall', traditionally associated with Macbeth and King Duncan's death. Any connection, as at Cawdor Castle, seems to be only based on Shakespeare's Scottish play: Glamis is not mentioned until 1264, more than 200 years after the event, and – anyway – Duncan was killed in battle near Elgin.

Glamis has long been held by the Lyon family, who were

given the lands by Robert II in 1372. The family became Earls of Strathmore and Kinghorne in the 17th century, and Elizabeth Bowes Lyon, the Queen Mother, was from the family.

One of the ghost stories goes back to the 16th century. Janet Douglas was the beautiful widow of John Lyon, 6th Lord Glamis, and – unfortunately for her – sister to Archibald Douglas, 6th Earl of Angus. Janet had a son, John, with her first husband, and later remarried, being wed to Walter Campbell of Skipness.

The king of the time, James V, was ill treated and imprisoned in his youth by the Earl of Angus, who had married his mother, Margaret Tudor, after the death of James IV in 1513 at the disastrous battle of Flodden. James V accused the Earl of Angus of treason, and then Janet of being in league with her brother. This might not have been enough to condemn her to death, so he added a plot to poison him using witchcraft. Janet, her son and her husband were seized at Glamis and then imprisoned in Edinburgh Castle in a lightless cell.

Although Janet conducted herself bravely and eloquently (despite being almost blind from the dark) she could not escape James's spite. She was found guilty and was burned alive on Castle Hill, now the Esplanade, at Edinburgh Castle on 3 December 1537. Her son would have also been executed, but he was too young for the sentence to be implemented, although he was reputedly forced to watch his mother being burned alive. Walter Campbell had tried to escape from the castle, but died in the attempt.

Janet's apparition, the Grey Lady of Glamis, is said to haunt where she was burned on the Esplanade, but to also have returned to Glamis. The tradition is that the bogle is seen mostly in the chapel and clock tower. In the chapel she is reported to have been witnessed several times, sitting or praying. In one account the ghost is described as a small figure through which the sun shone, leaving a pattern on the floor of the chapel. On another occasion the then Earl saw the ghost kneeling as if in prayer, and he withdrew. The Old Pretender, James Edward Stewart, visited the castle in 1716 during the Jacobite Rising, and the apparition was observed entering the chapel and then kneeling in prayer. James was, of course, the direct descendant of James V who had Janet executed.

James V died in 1542, before Janet's son John Lyon was old enough to be executed, and he was then pardoned and he retrieved his title and Glamis Castle, although it had been plundered in his absence.

Another famous ghost is that of either Alexander Lindsay, 4th Earl of Crawford, or Patrick Lyon, first Lord Glamis, who is said to haunt a walled-up room where he played cards with the devil. Here he is compelled to play until the 'day of doom'.

Alexander Lindsay, 'Earl Beardie', was certainly a cruel and ruthless character. Indeed, one story is that his mother smothered her own brother so that he would succeed to the Earldom of Crawford. It is said that Crawford's ghost can also be seen at the ruins of the castle of Lordscairnie, in Fife, on Hogmanay.

Other stories of ghosts and beasts abound and are widely reported, including that of the spirit of a little African boy, a White Lady, the ghost of a butler, the phantoms of a party of Ogilvies walled up somewhere in the castle, and even the spirit of a vampire serving girl, also bricked up in the building.

Open April-October, daily.

Tel: 01307 840393

Web: www.glamis-castle.co.uk

Glen More, Mull

On A849, 8 miles SW of Craignure, Mull, Argyll.

Through the middle of the beautiful island of Mull, and overlooked by the 3000-foot mountain Ben More, is Glen More. This is the main route to the holy isle of Iona with its renowned abbey and to the west of the island.

The island of Mull was long held by the MacLeans of Duart and the MacLaines of Moy. The splendid restored Duart Castle, home to the MacLeans, is located on the north-east tip of the island and is seen from the Oban ferry. The MacLeans used Loch Spelve as a haven for their birlinns or galleys. Moy Castle, a plain and somewhat stark tower, stands by the shore of the picturesque Loch Buie with its fine beach and was the seat of the MacLaines. Duart Castle is open to the public, and Moy can be viewed from the outside.

The ghost story goes back to events in the 16th century. Iain the Toothless was chief of the MacLaines, and his son and heir was Ewen of the Little Head. Ewen had been given an island dwelling in Loch Squabain as his residence, but his wife (always blame a woman!) did not feel that the house or marriage settlement was sufficient for their needs. This led to conflict between father and son, and eventually open battle. Their forces met in 1538, but it went badly for Ewen. At the outset of the fighting he was slain, his head being hewn off by an axe. His horse rode away down Glen More, his upright decapitated body still in the saddle, before coming to rest some two miles away.

Another element to the tale is the Bean-nighe, a spirit or supernatural being who presided over those about to die. The day before the battle Ewen encountered an old woman washing bloody shirts, the sarks of those who were to die in the morning. Ewen's was among them. A similar tale is

South of Mull from Glen More.

told of a girl who encountered a Bean-nighe one Sunday morning in Cromarty, again the creature was engrossed in washing and had many blooded shirts. It was not clear to what this could refer, as it was a time of peace, until the roof of Fearn Abbey fell in at worship, killing 36 souls.

Ewen's ghost, the headless horseman, is said to have been seen riding in Glen More when one of the MacLaines is about to die or suffer from a serious illness.

This harbinger of death is a common thread through many Scottish stories. There are many Green Ladies, Cortachy has its famous drummer, and there are also corporeal creatures such as white deer, a ram, a robin and a red-breasted swan. The Green Ladies would weep when something bad was to happen, but would also be happy when there was good news to come. They were also tied to the building or site, rather than to the family.

The story goes that the apparition of Ewen of the Little Head has been seen three times in living memory.

Access at all reasonable times.

Hermitage Castle

Off B6357, 5 miles N of Newcastleton, Borders, TD9 0LU.

Liddesdale, on the border between England and Scotland, was for many centuries an area of conflict, reiving and bloodshed. Most local lairds – Armstrongs, Elliots and Crosiers – built themselves castles and tower houses, but few of these survive except as shattered ruins. Apart from, that is, the grim old fortress of Hermitage.

Hermitage had several owners in its bloody history, and perhaps – not surprisingly – several ghosts.

In the 13th and early 14th centuries the castle was a property of the De Soulis family, who held lands on both sides of the border. William de Soulis was said to be a warlock and well versed in the black arts. Local children would disappear never to be seen again, and it was assumed that they were slaughtered within the walls and their blood used for all sorts of diabolic rituals. According to one account, the local people eventually took matters into their own hands and seized de Soulis. He was taken

to Ninestane Rig – a stone circle some 1.5 miles north-east of the castle – bound, wrapped in lead, and boiled in a cauldron. He may actually have been imprisoned in Dumbarton Castle for supporting the English, and the family were certainly forfeited in 1320 and lost the castle and lands.

Ghostly screams and cries have reportedly been heard from the victims of Lord Soulis, and his own ghost is said to haunt the castle and area around Hermitage. The stone circle certainly still exists, although it stands in a forestry plantation some distance from any road.

The castle later passed to the Douglases, one of the greatest of all Scottish families. William Douglas, 'The Knight of Liddesdale' and a devious fellow, was one of those who resisted Edward Balliol in the 1330s. He did, however, seize Sir Alexander Ramsay of Dalhousie at his devotions in St Mary's Church in Hawick. Ramsay was imprisoned in a dungeon at Hermitage, and starved to death, although a trickle of corn from a granary agonisingly prolonged his life.

Ramsay's spirit is said to have been seen and heard here, and his own castle of Dalhousie is also said to be haunted by several ghosts. In 1353 Douglas's own plotting caught up with him and he was ambushed and slain by his godson, another William, when he attempted to block the latter's promotion to the lordship of Douglas.

The castle did not stay with the Douglases, and in 1492 Archibald, 5th Earl of Angus, exchanged Hermitage for Bothwell in Clydesdale with Patrick Hepburn, Earl of Bothwell. The Douglases were heavily involved in the intrigues of the time, and James IV felt that the proximity to the border with England was just too much of a temptation.

As with many other castles in Scotland, Hermitage was visited by Mary Queen of Scots. In 1566 James Hepburn, 4th Earl of Bothwell, was involved in a fray and stabbed

by the Border reiver 'Little Jock' Elliot of Park: the latter was shot in the fight. Bothwell took some time to recover and was visited on his sick bed by Mary, Queen of Scots, although Mary made herself so unwell with the long ride that she nearly died when she returned to Jedburgh.

Mary and Bothwell were later married, although he was implicated in the murder of Darnley, her previous husband. Their marriage was a disaster: Mary was defeated in battle and fled to England, while he escaped to Norway. His end was not a happy one. He was incarcerated in the Danish fortress of Dragsholm and there died: his mummified corpse was on display until recently in a museum.

It is an apparition of Mary, in a white dress, that is said to haunt Hermitage, although her connection with the place is not strong so this is perhaps a mistaken identity.

Historic Scotland: open April-September, daily.

Tel: 01387 376222

Web: www.historic-scotland.gov.uk

Mary King's Close

Off A1, High Street (Royal Mile), Edinburgh, EH1 1PG.

Beneath the City Chambers on the Royal Mile is hidden a warren of streets where people, worked and died between the 17th and 19th centuries. The last resident Andrew Chesney was forced to leave in 1902, but only because of the compulsory purchase of his house.

The Real Mary King's Close consists of a number of underground closes, which would originally have been narrow alleys with houses on each side, climbing up to seven storeys high and dating back several centuries. In 1753 the burgh authorities decided to construct a grand new building, the Royal Exchange (now the City Chambers). The houses at the top of the closes were knocked down and levelled, but part of the lower sections were kept and used as foundations for the new building as it is on a steeply sloping site. A number of dark and mysterious underground closes and ancient dwellings were then entombed.

This intriguing underground site is also thought to be one of the most haunted places in Scotland.

One of the earliest and best documented concerns the legal agent, Thomas Coltheart, and his wife. The couple moved into Mary King's Close in 1685, after the close had been sealed up because of plague, and almost immediately their maidservant fled, claiming the place was haunted. Then on the Sabbath, the couple were accosted by visions of an old man's disembodied head floating in the air, a young child 'with its coat upon it', a severed arm appearing to beckon them, a ghostly dog running into the room followed by a cat, and the whole room being full of creatures 'dancing prettily'. The air was then filled with a dreadful groan and the all the apparitions disappeared. A few weeks later, having himself appeared in a vision to a friend, Thomas died.

Visitors to the close have reported scratching coming from inside a chimney where a young sweep is believed to have died. Sounds of a party or crowded tavern have also been reputedly been distantly overheard. Other recorded phantoms include a worried-looking man pacing the close, and a woman in black, identified by some as Mary King herself.

The strangest tale is that concerning the bogle of a little girl, who has come to be known as 'Annie'. A Japanese psychic, Aiko Gibo, visited the close, reportedly hardly able to enter the haunted room off Allan's Close because of the pain and unhappiness she felt there.

Eventually Gibo entered the chamber, and claimed to communicate with the young girl's spirit, saying that the wee girl was heartbroken because she had lost her mother and her favourite doll. Gibo then bought a doll to bring comfort to the wee girl's spirit, relating that Annie was absolutely delighted.

Since then visitors from all over the world have left Annie dolls and other toys, jewellery and even money, which is donated to the Sick Kids Friends Foundation.

General tour times (every 15 minutes): open all year, daily, except closed Christmas day. March-October open until 21.00. Also Dark Truth Tour (special one hour tour) all year, daily.

Tel: 0845 070 6244

Web: www.realmarykingsclose.com

Maryculter House

Off B9077, South Deeside Road, 8 miles SW of Aberdeen, AB12 5GB.

Picturesquely situated on the south bank of the Dee, not far from Aberdeen, is Maryculter House Hotel in five acres of woodland and landscaped gardens. It is substantially a 17th-century house of the Menzies family, later altered and extended, who held the property from 1535 or earlier. It

stands on the site of a preceptory of the Knights Templar. Vaulted cellars from the preceptor's house are built into the hotel, notably under the cocktail bar. The foundations of the nearby Templar's church and adjacent burial ground, which was used by the parish until 1782, can also be traced and are located opposite the reception car park.

The Knights Templar were a strict holy order of knights. They were dedicated to serving God and protecting pilgrims on their way to Jerusalem and the Holy Land during the times of the Crusades. They had several houses in Scotland, including one at Temple in Midlothian. A preceptory (akin to a priory) was founded here by Walter Bisset around 1230. The Templars became very powerful in Europe, and their order was eventually suppressed by the Pope in 1312.

The story goes that one of the Knights was Godfrey Wedderburn of Wedderhill. Godfrey went on Crusade to the Holy Land, where he distinguished himself, but he was badly wounded and had to be nursed back to health by a beautiful Saracen woman. Godfrey was a pious fellow and when he recovered he returned to Maryculter and the preceptory.

Years later the Saracen woman travelled to Scotland and looked for Godfrey. She found him at Maryculter. The preceptor (the head of the Order) did not believe that they were not lovers, or that Godfrey could be friendly with an enemy of the Church. Because the preceptor believed that Godfrey had broken his vows, Godfrey was forced to kill himself using his own dagger. The Saracen woman also plunged a knife into her own chest, but called down a curse on the preceptor. As she died a lightning bolt struck the Templar, and killed him, leaving a smoking hollow where he had been. This hollow, the 'Thunder Hole', which was formerly much deeper, can still be seen.

It is said that Godfrey and the Saracen were buried side by side, but that his apparition returns to ride over the hill of Kingcausie while the ghost of the beautiful Saracen woman has been seen in the woods. At least one account mentions a Green Lady, perhaps her bogle.

Hotel.

Tel: 01224 732124

Web: www.maryculterhousehotel.com

Meldrum House

Off A947, 1 mile N of Oldmeldrum, Aberdeenshire, AB51 0AE.

Set in fine landscaped parkland, Meldrum House is an impressive rambling mansion with tall round towers crowned by conical roofs at the corners. The building incorporates an ancient castle, dating from as early as the 13th century, but was altered down the centuries, including

by the removal of the uppermost storey. This was a property of the Meldrum family until about 1450, when it passed by marriage to the Setons (Alexander Seton, mentioned in the entry on Fyvie, came from this family), then from 1635 was owned by the Urquharts, then by the Duffs from 1898. The house is now used as a hotel and golf club.

The house is traditionally believed to be haunted by a Green Lady. More recent reports, however, have her clad in white, or this may be another ghost, of course…

Sightings of this apparition have been reported many times, as recently as 1985 when she reputedly gave a male guest a cold kiss during a thunder storm. She is also said to scratch the chests of men descended from any of the families who owned Meldrum when they occupy Room 3, the chamber with which she is most associated. Another account has the apparition being seen walking along an upstairs corridor.

In many accounts the ghost is named as the spirit of Isabella Douglas, who married William Urquhart of Meldrum in 1758, and whose portrait hangs in the hotel. Some claim that she was murdered.

The phantom is said to sometimes be seen moving in different ways: when it walks quickly or seems restless it is believed to be unhappy, when it glides about slowly it is reputed to be content. Although what would displease or please a disembodied entity is uncertain…

The ghost is also believed to be caring. There are stories that she visits children left alone in their rooms, who then reported that a lady in a white dress had been looking after them.

Hotel.

Tel: 01651 872294

Web: www.meldrumhouse.co.uk

Montrose Air Station Museum

Off A92, Waldron Road, Broomfield, N end Montrose, Angus, DD10 9DB.

Montrose airfield was established in 1913, making it one of the oldest in the country, and five years later was used for training American pilots. In World War II many others were trained here, including Commonwealth, Polish, Czech, American, Russian, Turkish and the Free French. The airfield was bombed by German bombers in 1940, and hangers and a mess were destroyed. The airfield was abandoned by the RAF in 1957.

A museum, housed in the HQ building, displays wartime memorabilia, comprising historic photographs, uniforms, mementoes and archive material, and is being expanded. Aircraft are also on display, including a Seahawk 131 and a replica Sopwoth Camel as well as a Bofors gun, a Commer airfield control van and Whirlwind XJ723. There is access to a war-time pillbox.

The aerodrome is said to be haunted. There are several

reports of a phantom biplane here, thought to be from a crash which happened soon after the airfield was opened Lieutenant Desmond Arthur of the Royal Flying Corps died in the crash in May 1913, and the sightings of the apparition of an airman, again recorded several times, are thought to be associated with the event. Desmond's recklessness was initially blamed for the crash in an official investigation, which may explain the appearance of his restless bogle, but when he was exonerated of all blame in 1916 the phantom was only seen one more time. Or at least until the outbreak of World War II.

Other manifestations include the unexplained sounds of footsteps and mumbled conversations from around the buildings, the phantoms of ghostly airmen wearing flying suits and goggles, and the apparition of a black labrador dog which follows people about.

On one occasion, an old radio on display, but with no power or aerial, is said to have begun broadcasting speeches by Winston Churchill and music from the Glen Miller Orchestra.

Open all year: April-October, Wednesday-Sunday; November-March, Sundays only; parties and other times by arrangement.

Tel: 01674 678222

Web: www.rafmontrose.org.uk

New Lanark

Off A73, 1 mile S of Lanark, New Lanark, ML11 9DB.

Surrounded by native woodlands and close to the famous Falls of Clyde, this iconic 200-year old World Heritage Site has been carefully restored as a living community, with an

award-winning Visitor Centre and Hotel, attracting over 400,000 visitors a year.

Long famed as a beauty spot, the waters of the Clyde were used from the 1780s for cotton mills, established by David Dale and Richard Arkwright. Robert Owen married Caroline Dale, David's daughter, and Owen believed that the excesses of the time should be countered by fair wages, affordable food, health care, education with no child labour and corporal punishment, although he expected hard work, abstinence and moderation in return. Owen showed that better work conditions could be combined with profits, a radical concept which appears to have lost favour in recent years. The history of the village is brought to life in a ride in motorised pods called the 'Annie McLeod Experience'.

The New Lanark Mill, now a hotel, was originally an 18th-century cotton mill, and has many original features including Georgian windows and barrel-vaulted ceilings, with fine views of either the River Clyde or the village.

Apparitions have been seen throughout the village. One particular house, located above the Village Store, is reputedly haunted by the bogle of a black-haired young woman dressed in a tartan cloak. She has been witnessed by children on different occasions, and is said to have disappeared through a sealed door.

Another account has a phantom of Robert Owen being seen seated at his desk and also looking out of a window of the house he formerly occupied.

Other manifestations from round New Lanark include unexplained bangs, thumps and footsteps, the crying and laughing of children, as well as the sightings of many other phantoms. One of the most intriguing is security camera footage from May 2010 of a car park in the village, with images of a white shifting apparition recorded for about 1.5 hours.

Access to village at all times. Visitor centre open all year, daily except closed Christmas Day and New Year's day. Hotel and self-catering accommodation.

New Lanark Visitor Centre: 01555 661345

Web: www.newlanark.org

New Lanark Mill Hotel: 01555 667200

Web: newlanarkhotel.co.uk

ROSSLYN CHAPEL

Off A701, in Roslin, 6 miles S of Edinburgh, EH25 9PU.

Situated near the sylvan wooded Roslin Glen and overlooking the River Esk is the magnificent Rosslyn Chapel. The chapel, dedicated to St Matthew and probably

intended as a collegiate church, was founded by William Sinclair (or St Clair), Earl of Orkney, in 1446. It was never completed: only the choir and parts of the transepts were built. The roof is vaulted and there are a mass of flying buttresses to carry the weight. Nevertheless it is an exceptional building.

The chapel is richly and exuberantly carved with Biblical stories, and has the largest number of 'Green Men' found in any medieval building. In the burial vault, beneath floor level, are ten of the Sinclairs of Rosslyn and their kin, once said to be laid out in full armour without coffins.

Ghostly flames were said to be seen here when one of the Sinclairs was about to die.

In recent years the chapel has been linked by some authors to the Holy Grail, as well as to the Knights Templar.

Rosslyn Chapel.

This latter association is somewhat speculative, however, as the Knights Templars were suppressed in 1312 and the chapel was not begun until the middle of the 15th century. William Sinclair, the chapel's builder, was reputedly Grand Master of the Knights Templar, who were by now an 'underground organisation'. The chapel and castle both feature in the 2006 movie of Dan Brown's *The Da Vinci Code* with Tom Hanks.

The chapel is reputedly haunted by the ghost of the apprentice, who carved the famous Apprentice Pillar and according to tradition was murdered by his teacher. The apparition of a monk has also been reported in recent times, both in the chapel and outside the building.

Rosslyn Castle.

In a very scenic and atmospheric spot above the River Esk, Rosslyn Castle is close by and is also said to be haunted. One story dates from the Wars of Independence in 1303, when an English army was heavily defeated by the Scots, led by John Comyn and Simon Fraser, near the castle. A spectre of a dog, the 'Mauthe Dog', killed with its English master after the battle, reputedly haunts the castle, and howling has been reported on several occasions.

Sir William Sinclair was one of the knights who set out on crusade with Robert the Bruce's heart, and was killed fighting the Moors in Granada in 1330. Bruce's heart was returned to Scotland and is buried at Melrose Abbey.

Rosslyn Castle was once a powerful and stately pile, with one of the most impressive entrances to any Scottish castle, and the Sinclairs had a large princely court. Rosslyn was, however, besieged, plundered and partly destroyed by Cromwell in 1650, after which it was never fully rebuilt, although part is still habitable and may be rented as holiday accommodation through the Landmark Trust.

Rosslyn Castle.

Nevertheless, a wondrous treasure is said to be buried beneath the vaults of the castle. This is guarded by a White Lady, said to be the bogle of one of the Sinclairs. The legend goes that she can only be woken and the treasure discovered if a trumpet is sounded when standing on the correct step on one of the staircases. As these rise some five storeys, and the lower two floors of the castle are not accessible (because of pigeons, not ghouls), this may prove problematic.

A further story is that of an apparition of a knight in black armour, riding a black horse, said to have been seen on at least three occasions in recent times.

Rosslyn Chapel: open all year, daily.

Tel: 0131 440 2159

Web: www.rosslynchapel.com

Roxburghe Hotel

Off A698, 3 miles S of Kelso, Borders, TD5 8JZ.

Situated near Kelso in the Borders is the Roxburghe Hotel. The building was formally known as Sunlaws, and dates mostly from 1853 after the previous house was destroyed

by fire. It stands in a tranquil location in 200 acres of gardens and wooded park land. It was a property of the Kerrs of Chatto, and Bonnie Prince Charlie was entertained here in November 1745. The house was used to hold German prisoners of war during World War II, was acquired by the Duke of Roxburghe in 1969, and is now an exclusive hotel.

The massive stately home of Floors Castle, still the seat of the Duke and Duchess of Roxburghe, is nearby and open to the public. Floors is said to be haunted by the ghost of a gardener, who is 'experienced', rather than seen, outside the main entrance.

The Roxburghe Hotel has several ghosts stories.

One concerns the apparition of a woman, a Grey Lady, who is said to be clad in grey. She walks the area on the ground floor, covering the corridor from the kitchen, through to the inner hall and then along the path leading out from the conservatory up to the Japanese bridge.

The story goes that she is searching for her baby, but there is no clue to her identity. The ghost has been seen several times in living memory.

Another ghost is reputedly that of a soldier. The apparition may be one of those imprisoned here during the war or one of the family who formerly lived at the house, as many of them were in the military. The ghost has been witnessed on the top floor of the house, which is currently only used for storage space. The apparition is dressed in brown, military-style clothing.

A third manifestation is felt rather than seen, and one of the rooms has had a strange aura from time to time. In 1990 a guest reported that she awoke suddenly at night with a strange sensation as if something cool was brushing down her entire body.

The administration offices, housed in the old laundry in the oldest part of the building, are also said to be haunted.

Hotel.

Tel: 01573 450331

Web: roxburghe-hotel.net

SHIELDHILL CASTLE

Off B7016, 3 miles NW of Biggar, Quothquan, Lanarkshire, ML12 6NA.

Set in the rolling hills and farmlands of the Upper Clyde Valley, Shieldhill Castle incorporates an old stronghold, parts of which date back to 1199. This was a property of the Chancellor family for hundreds of years. The family supported Mary Queen of Scots and fought for her at the Battle of Langside in 1568. Unfortunately this put them on the losing side, and their castle of Quothquan was burnt to the ground – so much so that no trace remains. The Chancellors only left Shieldhill in the 1950s, and since 1959 Shieldhill has been a country house hotel. Some of the rooms have four poster beds, and the building was bought in 2011 and completely renovated.

The building is said to be haunted by a Grey Lady, the ghost of the young and good-looking daughter of one

of the Chancellor lords. The bogle is said to be seen wrapped in a grey cloak.

There are several brutal or tragic versions of the story in various books and websites recorded down the years.

One is that the poor girl was raped by soldiers returning from a battle in the 1650s, and became pregnant, but the child was cruelly taken from her at birth and left to die (and that she was driven to suicide in grief). Another that she was made pregnant by a gamekeeper's son, and her baby was born dead then buried without her permission. The girl wept herself to death. A third that she fell to her death while trying to elope with her lover, a gamekeeper, or yet another that her father forbad her to see the fellow and in despair she committed suicide.

Whatever her origin, the tale goes that her ghost has been seen in recent times, walking towards the burial place in the grounds of the hotel, but especially in one of the rooms, now part of the Glencoe Suite. She is mostly seen (or experienced) on the top floor of the old keep but, tis said, uses the original stone stair to move from floor to floor. Unexplained footsteps and thumps during the night have also been reported, as have chairs moving by themselves and television channels changing independently.

There are also stories of a ghostly butler in the kitchen, where lights are said to have turned themselves on, manifestations having been witnessed in recent years.

Hotel.

Tel: 01899 220035

Web: shieldhillcastlehotel.co.uk

STIRLING CASTLE

Off A872, head of Stirling's historic old town, FK8 1EJ.

Stirling is one of the most important, imposing and picturesque castles in Scotland. It stands on a rocky outcrop above the old burgh of Stirling, and its location is near a strategic crossing of the Forth. Two important battles in

the Wars of Independence were fought nearby: Stirling Bridge, when William Wallace crushed an English army in 1297, and Bruce's famous victory at Bannockburn in 1314.

This was a very strong castle, but was also a royal palace and much was built or rebuilt by James IV, James V and James VI. There are many fine Renaissance features, and the Royal Apartments are being refurbished to their medieval appearance with tapestries, furniture and decorative details.

The castle has a long and fascinating history, and was the scene of many a dark deed. Perhaps the most notorious was the savage murder in 1452 of William Douglas, 8th

Earl of Douglas, by the king James II and his followers. Douglas had been promised safe conduct, but he was set upon, cruelly slain, and then his body was contemptuously thrown out of a window.

There are several ghost stories associated with the castle.

During renovation work on the Great Hall there were reports of ghostly footsteps coming from the roof. Unexplained footsteps have also been heard in the Governor's Block and the King's Old Building, apparently climbing stairs that no longer exist and pacing the length of a passageway which has been divided.

Stirling reputedly has both a Green and a Pink Lady. The Green Lady, an apparition clad in a green frock, is said to be a herald of misfortune, especially when there is about to be a fire. One report has this ghost so terrifying a cook in the old kitchen that the poor man fainted.

The Pink Lady is the phantom of a beautiful girl, seen both in the castle and as far away as the Church of the Holy Rude. Some say she is the spirit of Mary, Queen of Scots; others that she lost her husband in a siege of the castle in 1304.

The kilted apparition of a man has also been reported, and a photograph of this ghost was taken in 1935. This bogle is apparently the most reported, and has been mistaken for a costumed castle guide, before vanishing.

Historic Scotland Open all year, daily.

Tel: 01786 450000

Web: www.stirlingcastle.gov.uk

TIBBIE SHIEL'S INN

Off A708, 1.5 miles S of Cappercleuch, St Mary's Loch,
Borders, TD7 5LH.

Hidden away in a place of peace and beauty is Tibbie Shiel's
Inn. It is located on an isthmus between the tranquil
St Mary's Loch and Loch of Lowes, south of Peebles in the
Borders. The establishment was opened in 1823 by Isabella
Shiel – also known as Tibbie. Tibbie's husband, Robert
Richardson, a mole catcher, had died, and she was
penniless and left with six children, so she opened her
house to take in lodgers. The inn grew in popularity and

was visited by her friend James Hogg, the Ettrick Shepherd,
who wrote the *Private Memoirs and Confessions of a Justified
Sinner*, and other writers and poets. Guests included Sir
Walter Scott, Robert Louis Stevenson, the publisher Robert
Chambers, and Thomas Carlyle.

Tibbie died in 1878 at the ripe old age of 96 and was
buried in Ettrick Kirkyard, where her husband also rests,
but the inn remained open. The building has been extended
over the years.

St Mary's Loch.

The inn is believed to be haunted by Tibbie's ghost. Manifestations include a cold hand on the shoulder, but it is thought that Tibbie is only keeping a watchful eye on her establishment. A report of the ghost was recorded in one of the bedrooms in 1996.

The ghost of a dog has also been experienced, felt rather than seen. The story goes that it belonged to a guest who died while away from the inn. The dog pined away after the death of its owner.

Inn.

Tel: 01750 42231

Web: tibbieshiels.com

Traquair House

Off B709, 1 mile S of Innerleithen, Borders, EH44 6PW.

One of the oldest continuously inhabited houses in Scotland, Traquair House is a magnificent castle and mansion set in fine landscaped policies by the River Tweed. The building incorporates an ancient tower house, which

may date from as early as the 12th century. There are many furnished rooms, and the remains of 17th-century painted ceilings. There are also Jacobite and Stewart mementoes, including a crucifix and rosary belonging to Mary, Queen of Scots.

Alexander I had a hunting lodge here, and Traquair was visited by many of the kings of Scots, and some of England: Edward I and Edward II in the 14th century during the Wars of Independence. Traquair passed through several families until sold to the Stewart Earls of Buchan in 1478. The family supported the Stewart monarchs through thick and thin. Mary, Queen of Scots, visited with Lord Darnley in 1566 when pregnant with the future James VI. She left behind a quilt, said to have been embroidered by herself and her four Marys. John, 4th Laird, was one those who helped her escape from Lochleven Castle in 1568 and was captain of her bodyguard, but she was soon defeated at Langside and fled to England. At Traquair is the bed, rescued from Terregles, where she spent some of her last nights on Scottish soil.

Bonnie Prince Charlie visited the house on his way south in 1745 to invade England. He entered Traquair through the famous Bear Gates. The story goes that Charles, 5th Earl, closed and locked them after Charlie's departure, swearing they would not be unlocked until a Stewart once more sat on the throne of the country. They are still locked, of course, and Earl was imprisoned after the Rising.

By no means all ghosts stories had a tragic event as their origin, and indeed some spirits seem to linger because they

Kings Room, Traquair House.

loved the place they haunt. At Traquair it is the grounds that are believed to be occasionally visited by a bogle.

The apparition of Lady Louisa Stewart, sister of the 8th and last Earl of Traquair, is reported to have been sighted going on her favourite walk by the Quair in the policies of Traquair. She lived to a fine old age, dying in 1875 when she was 100 years old. Her portrait hangs in the house.

Open April-October, daily; November, Saturday and Sunday only. Accommodation. Brewery.

Tel: 01896 830323

Web: traquair.co.uk

Tulloch Castle Hotel

Off A862, 1 mile N of Dingwall, Tulloch, Ross and Cromarty, IV15 9ND

Tulloch Castle is a large and impressive building, parts of which may date from the 12th century. It incorporates a square keep with a round stair-tower at one corner. The first-floor chambers of the building have ornate plaster ceilings and the great hall has 250-year-old panelling,

Like many other castles, Tulloch is believed to have had a secret passageway to another stronghold, in this case linking it to Dingwall Castle (the site of which is about a mile to the south). Part of the tunnel has collapsed, and this can be seen in the middle of the front lawn.

The Vikings may have had a stronghold here, and the lands were held by a Fergus Oure in 1500, but passed to the Innes family in 1526 and then the Bains until 1762. Tulloch then

went to the Davidsons, who were related by marriage, and they held it until 1945: several of them were Provosts of Dingwall. The building was used as a hospital during World War II, then as a school, but it is now a hotel.

Tulloch is one of the many castles which are said to have a Green Lady, reportedly the bogle of Elizabeth Davidson, the daughter of one of the owners. The story goes that the girl was upstairs when she surprised her father, who was in a compromising clinch with a woman who was not the daughter's mother. The girl was so appalled that she fled the chamber, but in her consternation tripped, fell down the stairs and was killed. A portrait which hangs in the castle is believed to be of the girl in life.

Her ghost, clad in green, has been reported in the building, along with other manifestations, and the bar is named after her. She is said to have been witnessed many times when the building was used as a hospital.

The apparition of a maid is also recorded, said to have been seen in the Pink Room, as well as the phantom of a previous owner in the hall, where other uncanny manifestations are said to happen. These have also been reported in Room 8, where a guest gave an account of being pinned into his bed, and also including doors closing by themselves, changes in temperature, and unexplained knocking.

A photograph was taken on the stairs in 2008 which appears to show an apparition below the photographer on the steps with its hand on the bannister.

Hotel.

Tel: 0843 178 7143

Web: www.bespokehotels.com/tullochcastlehotel